'*A person's life is just a moment in infinity*'

LEONARDO DA VINCI

Leonardo was born in 1452 in Vinci, near Florence.

When he was twenty, he painted an angel so beautifully that he surpassed his teacher, Verrochio.

After that, he painted many portraits, and a battle scene too.

He drew madonnas and saints.

But he also drew the faces of ordinary people, beautiful and ugly alike.

And he drew animals, real ones and ones that he just imagined.

He studied nature, especially plants.

He watched the wind and the waves

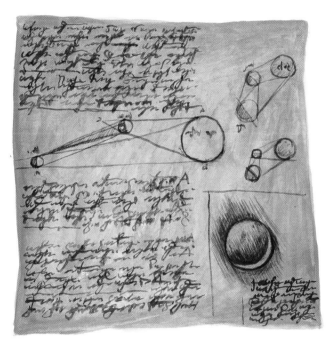

as well as the sun, the moon and the sky.

He studied the earth and the cosmos.

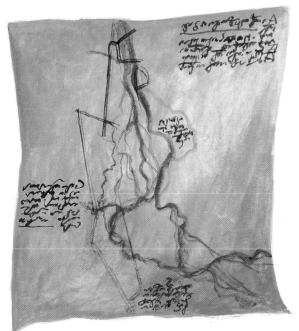

He drew cities and rivers seen from above,

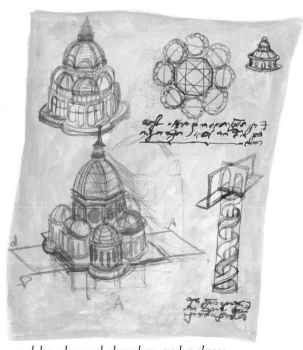

and he planned churches and palaces…

Barefoot Books
PO Box 95
Kingswood
Bristol
BS30 5BH

This book was typeset in Bembo

Typesetting by Design Principals, Wiltshire
Colour separation by Color Gallery, Singapore
Printed and bound in Singapore by Tien Wah Press (Pte) Ltd

This book has been printed on 100% acid-free paper

ISBN 1 84148 300 1

British Cataloguing-in-Publication Data: a catalogue record for this book is available from
the British Library

1 3 5 7 9 8 6 4 2

THE GENIUS OF

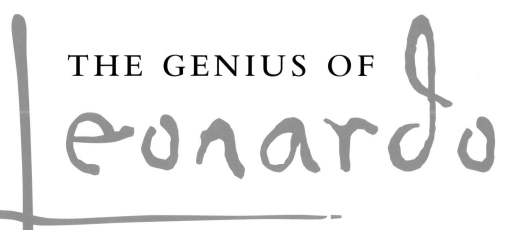

Leonardo

written by Guido Visconti

with quotations, some abridged, from the notebooks of Leonardo da Vinci

illustrated by Bimba Landmann

walk
the way of wonder...
Barefoot Books

The first rays of sun had not yet appeared in the east, but Giacomo was already up. He was on his way to fetch the milk for his master, Leonardo, when he came across a bird that had hurt its wing. Giacomo picked it up. He knew that his master would know how to heal the bird, because he stayed up every night studying the wings of bats. His house was full of them. He was using them as models for the flying machine that he was designing. He had given Giacomo strict instructions not to touch his machine, but Giacomo had taken no notice and touched it anyway, just a day ago. Leonardo was furious with him. He even wrote this on a piece of paper:

1490. Giacomo has come to live with me. He is ten years old. He is a liar, a thief and a greedy brute.

He also wrote: *He eats as much as two boys and causes as much trouble as four.*
Giacomo was very upset when he read this. He decided that from now on,
he would make an effort to be good. He did not want Leonardo to send
him away. He loved working for him and he knew that he was an
important person. Everyone said that he was a genius, even Ludovico il
Moro, the duke of Milan, who employed Leonardo.

Giacomo did not really know what a genius was, but he knew that his
master was cleverer than anyone else. Leonardo was always inventing new
machines, like the one for walking on water. He could play the harp; he
could write forwards or backwards, using his left hand as well as his right;
and above all he could paint. He could even paint people he had never
seen, like the Virgin Mary and her mother, Saint Anne.

At that moment, Leonardo was painting a real woman, whose name was Mona Lisa. It was always fun when she arrived, because Leonardo called in musicians and clowns to keep her happy while she was posing. Perhaps that was why she had such a sweet smile.

Today, Leonardo was painting this mysterious smile on to his canvas.

'Why aren't you painting her jewellery as well?' asked Giacomo.

'*A beautiful face attracts more attention than rich ornaments. And it is more valuable to show what is inside a person's soul,*' Leonardo replied.

'Well, why are you painting a landscape in the background that doesn't exist?' Giacomo wanted to know.

In fact, he really loved that landscape. And he was not the only one to wonder how Leonardo managed to paint valleys and mountains seen from above. After all, he had not yet built his flying machine. Only the eagles could see like that — everyone said so.

Leonardo waited until Mona Lisa had left, then he explained:

'*A painter is a bit like God. He can create whatever he wants to see, whether they're scary things or funny things. If he wants to see a cool place when the weather is hot, or a hot place when the weather is cold, he can do it. In the same way, he can look at the countryside and the sea as if he were on the top of a mountain.*'

'In that case, I want to be a painter too!' laughed Giacomo.

Leonardo laughed with him. '*Many people would like to become painters. But they draw like children, without showing the shadows of things,*' he said.

Giacomo did not understand. What did his master mean by 'shadows'? Objects only had one shadow, which you could see when the sun came out. Why should anyone want to draw that, he wondered.

But he wanted to understand. So when Leonardo's students arrived the next morning, he did not go and tend to their horses. Instead, he stayed in the studio to eavesdrop. He could hear his master teaching:

'There are shadows which are clear, and shadows which are dark, according to the intensity of the light. The light that illuminates an object may come from the sun, or the moon, or the flame of a candle…'

Although Giacomo could hear everything, he soon stopped listening. Something interesting had caught his eye. The sun was gleaming on a beautiful silver box on the table. The box had not been there the day before. Giacomo wanted to steal it, but from the easel Mona Lisa seemed to be watching him with her strange smile, as if to say, 'I can see you!' Only when Leonardo stepped in front of the picture and hid that smile did he snatch the box…

He ran off to the stables with it, to hide it under the straw. But he stopped in his tracks. He was sure something was moving inside the box. What could it be? Was it a bat? Or something else? Very, very slowly he opened the box — and let out a scream: 'Help! It's a dragon!'

Leonardo heard the scream and came running in, roaring with laughter. His joke had worked! He knew that Giacomo would not be able to resist stealing the box, so that he could sell it and buy himself some sugared almonds, as he had done before. So Leonardo had put a lizard in the box, with the crest of a cockerel attached to its head and two bat wings glued to its sides.

Leonardo was delighted that he had given his little thief such a fright! When the other servants came out, everyone wondered how he could put up with such a little demon in his house.

'It's because he is good looking, so Leonardo uses him as a model when he wants to paint angels,' said some.

'It's because he wants to understand everything, even the character of naughty children,' said others.

But this time, Leonardo did not scold Giacomo. Instead, he scolded himself for having frightened the lizard.

'Whoever fails to respect the lives of others does not deserve his own life,' he muttered to himself as he took off the false wings and set the creature free. Then, out of the blue, he told Giacomo to follow him to the market.

Giacomo was not at all surprised. His master was always doing this kind of thing. Whenever something came into his head, he had to do it straight away. And the lizard had reminded him of other little prisoners for sale in the market.

Just as he had on many other days, Leonardo bought all the caged birds. He could not bear seeing the freest creatures on Earth deprived of their freedom.

Leonardo waited until they were out of the city, then he opened the cages. And he told Giacomo, *'Birds hold their right or left wing lower, depending on which way they want to turn.'*

'That's true,' said Giacomo, watching one of the birds holding its wings close to its body as it swooped down.

'And birds never fly downwards tail first, because their centre of gravity is closer to the head than to the tail,' added Leonardo, but Giacomo found this a bit too difficult to understand. He was much more interested in Leonardo's flying machine. His master had told him that one day, thanks to his flying machine, people would be able to fly through the air, just like birds. Perhaps Giacomo would be able to, when he was older — that would be really wonderful.

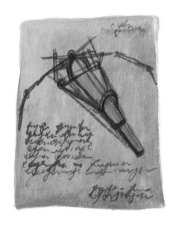 

It would also be wonderful to be able to spend a day in a city like the one that Leonardo was planning. He called it 'the ideal city'. Perhaps it would remain only a dream. The plans were almost finished, though, and Giacomo could easily imagine it, with high roads where carts could not go, and low roads just for the carts and the beasts of burden. It would be a clean city, because there were underground waterways where all the rubbish could be thrown away. Nothing dirty would be put in the canals. And Leonardo had said, *'Whoever wants to travel over all the earth by the high roads may do so, and the same goes for those who want to travel by the low ones.'*

'Over all the earth?' Giacomo wondered. 'He must mean over all the city, because he loves the earth far too much to want to cover it with roads.'

Now that all the birds were free, he could see just how much Leonardo loved nature. He was bending down to examine flowers; gathering leaves; making sketches; taking notes. He wanted to understand everything; he was fascinated by everything. He also wanted to rouse Giacomo's curiosity, and he bet his young assistant that he did not know how to calculate the age of trees. Of course, Giacomo had no idea!

'The rings on a sawn tree trunk indicate the number of years for which it has grown, and the width of each circle tells you whether the year was a wet or a dry one,' explained Leonardo.

That was really interesting, but then Giacomo wanted to know how to calculate the age of a bat, or a frog, or a horse, or a person he did not know...

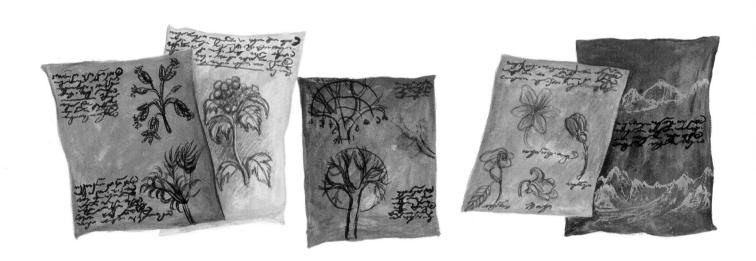

But for some reason, Leonardo did not answer his questions. It was obvious that he was listening to something, because his head was cocked to one side, only it was not Giacomo — it was another sound, far off in the distance... Giacomo cocked his head too. Yes, he could hear the pounding of horses' hooves, far, far away, and he could feel the ground trembling.

A long column of soldiers was heading their way. They were the soldiers of the King of France, who wanted to conquer the rich duchy of Milan.

Giacomo was overcome with excitement. He had never seen soldiers before and he would have liked to run and meet them. But Leonardo was angrier than he had ever seen him before. He turned straight back towards the city:

'War! What barbaric madness!' he kept muttering.

In the city, the soldiers were everywhere, and Leonardo was in full fury:
'Ever since men have appeared on this earth, they have done nothing but fight each other.
What a foul breed of animals they are!'

Unfortunately, the soldiers did not only fight one another. They destroyed everything, even the clay horse that stood in the courtyard of Duke Ludovico's castle. Leonardo was in despair. He had modelled that horse himself, to cast it in bronze and make from it the greatest equestrian statue in the world…

But now the statue could never be made, Duke Ludovico told him one morning. The bronze was needed for cannons.

These were terrible times for everyone, including Leonardo.
He stopped painting.
He stopped going to the market to buy caged birds.
He stopped going to the countryside to gather plants.
He stopped designing his flying machine.
Instead he designed weapons, cannons and fortifications for Duke Ludovico.
Giacomo knew that people had to defend themselves against their enemies, but he was still surprised to see Leonardo designing weapons.
'Why do you do it, if you hate war?' he asked.
'I do it to preserve nature's most precious gift — and that gift is our freedom,' Leonardo answered gravely.

Then one day, Duke Ludovico came to give Leonardo some good news. He had asked the prior at the convent of Santa Maria delle Grazie to find work for Leonardo. The prior had agreed. 'A large fresco on the wall of our refectory would be just the thing,' he said. So Leonardo could start painting again.

But he did not paint a fresco. To make a fresco, you have to work in a hurry, on fresh plaster. Once the plaster is dry, it is impossible to retouch the painting. No! Leonardo spent months, even years, on his paintings. He had to be able to alter and improve them as he went along. So he needed a different technique, one that would enable him to work slowly.

'A wall painted in tempera?' exclaimed the astonished prior when Leonardo began to mix his colours. 'But…are you sure the paint will last? It won't dry up and flake off?'

The prior was full of doubts. Leonardo did not know whether the paint would last. He only knew that with tempera he could adjust his colours. He could add a detail here and alter an expression there at any moment.

'At any moment…' snorted Giacomo when Leonardo insisted on riding over to the friars' refectory at dawn, just to add one more brushstroke before leaving again.

But although he teased his master, Giacomo really loved the painting.

Leonardo had said that a refectory needed something special. So he painted Jesus and his apostles eating together. It is the last time Jesus will ever eat with them and he has just said, 'One of you will betray me.' The apostles are agitated. You can tell from their gestures and the way they draw back, as if to say, 'One of us?' 'Did you hear that?' 'It's impossible!' 'Not I, that's for sure!'

The prior was full of admiration when he saw the painting. 'I feel as if I am there with them, at their last supper together,' he said.

And, just like the prior, many, many people came to see and praise the work.

One day, even Francis I came, the young king of France. He stood in front of the picture all morning.

Giacomo overheard him negotiating with the prior. 'This piece is too fine to stay in a convent. I want to take it back to France. I want to dismantle the wall. I want…'

But even kings cannot always have what they want. How could the wall be moved without ruining the picture?

King Francis was not going to be put off, so he approached Leonardo.

'Mon père, venez à ma cour. Vous y serez respecté, aimé…'

'What is he saying?' Giacomo asked one of the friars.

'He has invited Leonardo to go to the French court, where he will be given the love and respect he deserves…'

'Aha!' said Giacomo. 'The king cannot take away the wall, so he will take away Leonardo instead!'

Leonardo hesitated for a long time, but in the end he decided to accept the French king's invitation.

It was a brave decision for a man of his age. He had to leave everything: his home, his friends, and his country.

But he did not leave his painting of Mona Lisa. The king wanted to buy it, but to ensure that he would not be separated from it, Leonardo said that it was not yet finished.

In France, he was full of plans. He wanted to build canals to link the Loire, the great river which ran past the king's castle, to the other great rivers of France. He wanted to drain the marshes, and build his ideal city there…

But these projects were very expensive, and the king could not afford them.

Instead, he asked Leonardo to organise his parties. Leonardo had always excelled at this, making elaborate costumes and creating wonderful special effects for everyone to marvel at.

One day, he made a golden lion for a festival. At first, the guests were disappointed. 'Is that all?' they asked each other. Then, when the lion walked by itself to the king's throne, and when a mass of white lilies fell from its stomach as if by magic, everyone was speechless.

'How did he do that? Really, there cannot be anyone in the world who knows as much as Leonardo,' announced the king, as his guests looked on in astonishment.

'Yes, Leonardo does know a lot, but there's one thing he doesn't know,' thought Giacomo when he and his master stopped late that night to look at the stars. Giacomo asked him why the moon never falls from the sky. Leonardo could not give him an answer. He had often asked the same question: *'The moon is so heavy and dense; how does it stay up there?'*

But even if he didn't know everything, Giacomo still thought that Leonardo deserved the king's compliments, and he said so.

Leonardo smiled, and he explained that a person's life is just a moment in infinity. During that moment, no one can do and know all that they would like. He told Giacomo to put a stick in the water. Then he explained, *'The water that you are touching in the river is like the end of the moment that has just passed, but it is also the beginning of the moment that has just started. That is what time is like.'*

Giacomo was not sure that he understood this. But he was sure that the art and the work of Leonardo would last for a long time, and that others would be able to accomplish what he had only been able to start. 'And one day,' thought Giacomo, 'men will really be able to fly. Perhaps they will even be able to go and see what's up there, on the moon.'

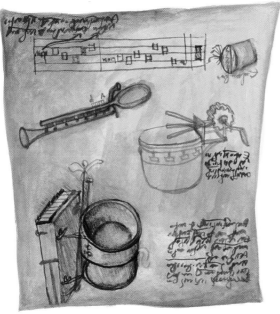

He played the lyre and designed many musical instruments.

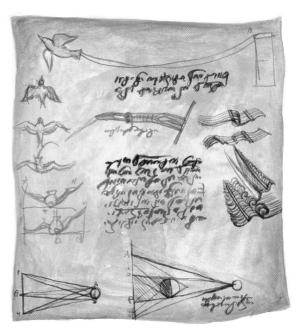

He wrote about light and shadow, and about the flight of birds,

and he thought up stories and riddles.

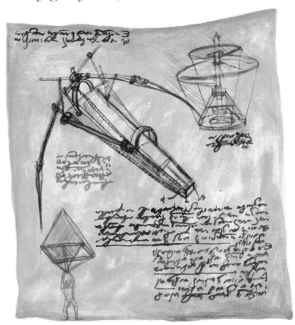

He invented machines for flying,

and for walking on water,

and a splendid carriage, the ancestor of the car.

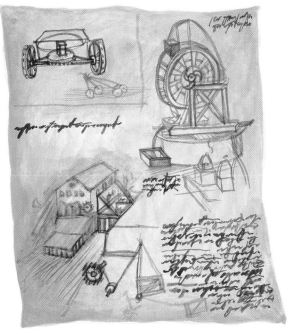

He studied wells, lock gates, and water wheels,

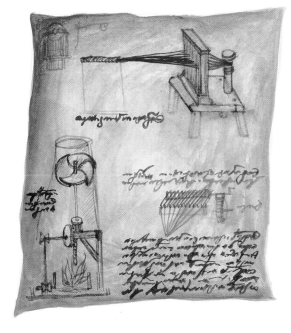

and mechanical roasting spits and looms,

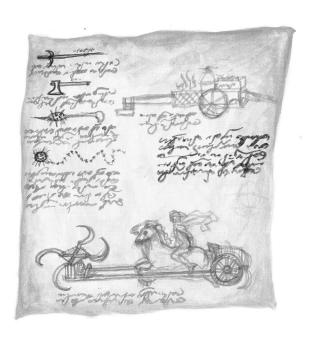

as well as weapons, 'to defend our freedom'.

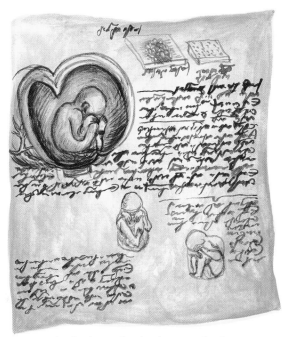

He looked inside the human body, to understand the beginnings of life

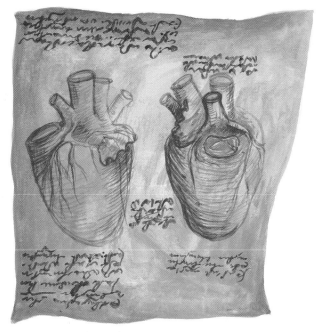

and to learn how the heart works.

Leonardo died in France, in 1519.

Extracts from Leonardo da Vinci's Manuscripts

walk
the way of wonder...
Barefoot Books

The barefoot child symbolizes the human being who is in harmony
with the natural world and moves freely across boundaries of many
kinds. Barefoot Books explores this image with a range of high-quality
picture books for children of all ages. We work with artists, writers and
storytellers from many cultures, focusing on themes that encourage
independence of spirit, promote understanding and acceptance of
different traditions, and foster a life-long love of learning.
www.barefoot-books.com